Did *God* Call Women to Preach the Gospel?

Rev. Dr. George A. Bates, JD

ISBN 979-8-88832-406-6 (paperback)
ISBN 979-8-88832-407-3 (digital)

Christian Faith Publishing
832 Park Avenue
Meadville, PA 16335
www.christianfaithpublishing.com

Printed in the United States of America

Acknowledgments

It is with deep appreciation to acknowledge the three women who perused this manuscript copiously and gave me their precious feedback. They are my friends, Rev. Dr. Christine Thomasson; Rev. Rene Jiggets-Tucker; and Ms. Jo Richenthaler, a former neighbor from Morehead City, North Carolina, who confided in me that it was her brother who read the pages to her. I would also like to thank those other women ministers and pastors who received the manuscript and did not respond to it. I can only deduce that what they read was not so alarming to warrant a response or what they read was too shocking to merit a reply. Rev. Jiggets-Tucker was the spiritual wind beneath my wings as she continuously inspired me to keep writing and refining the work. I would also like to thank the staff at the Carteret County Community College library for putting up with my many requests for assistance with my research and word-processing challenges.

Introduction

Let us examine this scripture in the context that it was delivered! In 1 Timothy 2:2–4, Paul exhorts "kings and all that are in authority" to "lead a quiet and peaceable life in godliness and honesty" (v. 2). Here comes a key statement in verse 3: "For this is good and acceptable in the sight of God our Savior: who will have all men (mankind) to be saved and to come unto the knowledge of the truth." God wants all men (mankind) should come to know the knowledge of truth, and He wants all of us to be saved, and He wanted godly men to lead us unto salvation! However, this verse implies that it was God's original intent that the man would be head of the household and leader in the church, but man's disobedience caused God to enact plan B, which offered leadership positions in the church to women! See the authority placed in King, Judge, and Prophetess Deborah in Judges 4:4 et seq., yet she was the godly wife of a man! Now if God did not see any confusion, fallacy, or ambiguity in this relationship, why has man imputed something "wrong" with this picture, that is, a godly woman with a godly husband being the judge, the king, and a prophet?

Chapter 2 invokes the "spirit" of Adam and Eve (vv. 13, 14) and reminds us that "Adam was not deceived, but the woman deceived was in the transgression" (v. 14).

1. It was always God's intent that the "obedient" children of Israel should spread the gospel of Jesus Christ throughout

the world! However, because of man's disobedience, Peter had to boldly throw the door open to the Gentiles (Acts 13:46).

2. God wanted Esau as the firstborn to be the "horn" of Israel, but he rightfully sold his birthright to Jacob for a bowl of porridge!

3. After making some rules and regulations for true men of God, Apostle Paul turns the role of women in the church (v. 9) and remarks, "In like manner also, that women adorn themselves in modest apparel, with shamefacedness and sobriety; not braided hair, or gold, or pearls, or costly array." "But (which becometh women professing godliness) with good works" (v. 10). "Let the woman learn in silence with all subjection" (v. 11). The last sentence was a Jewish custom that women should not lead men in the synagogue or temple! Doing so would send a mixed signal to men and women that the women may be held in subjection of the men! Not so!

4. Therefore, in verse 12 when Paul writes, "But I suffer not a woman to teach, nor to usurp authority over the man, but to be in silence," it must be read in the context that it was given—that is, women should be silent in the synagogue and not teach men in the temple for the reason stated in item 3 supra! There is no prohibition for women teaching women, and there is no prohibition of women teaching men in other places, but Paul does not want women to teach men in the synagogue for the reason stated in item 3 supra! As an addendum to this reasoning is the fact that Paul knew that all the "Jesus men" (him, the disciples, Mark, and others who were teaching the Gospel of Jesus Christ) were being hunted by the Roman soldiers! And all the Sanhedrin (the high priest) were "spies" for the Roman Empire—they were informants for the empire to save their necks and preserve their power base as the "supreme leaders of the Jews!" Jesus challenged the legendary authority of the high priest, the Sadducees, the Pharisees, and the

scribes as the "voice of God" as He told His disciples, "If you knew God [from the Old Testament], you should know Me!" (John 14:7). Then He goaded them a little with the conclusion: "How could you have known Me for all these years [about three and a half years of His earthly ministry] and not know that I am the Father and the Father is Me?" (John 14:9).

Now let us consider that when Paul is speaking and writing in chapter 2 of 1 Timothy, he knows about the authority placed in King Deborah by God Himself! Paul has been an altar boy working in the temple and assisting the high priest in their daily rituals since he was eight years old. He has been studying and being instructed by the high priests, who are of Pharisaic and Sadducean ancestry like himself, ever since that time! Paul knows that Ana the Prophetess blessed Jesus and has been a resident of the temple constantly in Jerusalem ever since her young husband died (Luke 2:37).

Paul knows that he and Phoebe (Romans 16) ran the Church at Ephesus together prior to God commissioning him to go on his first missionary journey! And when Paul left on his journey, Phoebe was left in charge of the Church at Ephesus, and she was more than the putative leader of this church. She was the pastor of this church, vis-á-vis, Paul directs all to "receive her in the Lord, as becometh saints, and that ye assist her in whatsoever business she hath need of you: for she hath been a succourer of many, and myself also!" (Romans 16:2).

Imagine that: Phoebe has led many to the throne of grace, and she has been a "succorer" of Paul himself! Even though Paul has been nominated by God to offer salvation to the Gentiles and be the defender of the Israelites (*apologesia*) against the Roman Empire, he also has been led in instruction by a woman named Phoebe! How can this be?

Romans 16:7 gives you the answer! Paul directs all the followers of Jesus Christ to "salute Andronicus and Junia, my kinsmen, and my fellow prisoners, who are of note among the apostles, who were in Christ before me." Paul does not say that the husband was in Christ before he and Andronicus had an obedient wife who was with the latter when he learned about Christ, but that both of them "were in Christ before him." And these people were known to him long before Paul's conversion on the road to Damascus because Andronicus and Junia were his kinsmen, probably his cousins! Likewise, look at all of the husband-and-wife teams who had churches in their homes and greet and bless all who are in their "households" (vv. 10, 11)!

I must note here that in the KJV, the word *households* is italicized, which would denote some coding going here! You must remember that at this time (AD 33 to Paul's death around AD 60), the Roman soldiers were hunting all of the "Jesus men" to kill them! So the followers of Christ could not use the word *church*, as that would have been a dead giveaway of a renegade religious sect among the Jews who were not sanctioned by the Sanhedrin! If you were not sanctioned by the Sanhedrin, then you were marked for death as this was the arrangement between the high priests and the Roman government of Governor Pontius Pilate and King Marcus Agrippa! The Sanhedrin was assisting the Roman soldiers to rid Jerusalem, the region of Samaria, and Judea of these troublesome Jesus men! In other words, the followers of Christ were being hunted as wanted men—dead or alive!

Herein lies a key reason God had already sanctioned women to do His work as God knew that there would come a time when the women would be crucial to carrying on Jesus's work as the men were being watched copiously by the high priests and the Roman soldiers!

For instance, after the hanging of our Lord and Savior Jesus Christ, who were still stirring about keeping watch on things and the body of Jesus? It was the three Marys—Mary, the mother of Jesus; Mary Magdalene; and Mary, the sister of Martha and Lazarus. And there was the beloved John; they were the chief followers of Christ whom the Roman army or the Sanhedrin paid no attention to! The Sanhedrin placed no value in women beyond procreation and household chores, and the Roman Empire had no respect for women as leaders and thinkers! Women were not to be educated in the Jewish faith or in the Roman Empire!

Roman women, as the wives of emperors, governors, kings, generals, colonels, and high-ranking officers, were allowed instruction in poetry and some language exercises, but no learning in history or the inner workings of the Roman senate or any other governmental entity! The gender bias of the day was their undoing because it was the women who survived the first century AD to make sure that Jesus's Gospel continues on in perpetuity! Now does this not all make perfect sense? God knows the fallacies, the weaknesses, the conniving, and the many plans of man (Proverbs 19:27) to "subvert, thwart, and subvert" His plan, and He has a maneuver for all of man's devilment that is eternal in the heavens! God knows that this day would come with us as players and/or actors for Him eons ago! Likewise, God knew before we entered into our mothers' wombs which one of us would be ministers, pastors, evangelists, and Bible teachers for Him because of Romans 8:28: "And we know that all things work together for good to them that love God, to them who are the called according to his purpose." Verses 29–31 make this point very plain: "For he did foreknow, he also did predestinate to be conformed to the image of his Son, that he might be the firstborn among many brethren. Moreover, whom he did predestinate, them he also called: and whom he called, them he also justified: and whom he justified, them he also glorified. What shall we then say to these things? If God be for us, who can be against us?"

(I must digress for a moment; these passages are completely ignored and disregarded by the Catholic Church, the Presbyterians, the Episcopalians, the Methodists, and the United Methodists—aka the Big Five—and their offspring as they do not submit to the theology that God calls you into the ministry, and the Godhead and He called you before you entered your mother's womb! *You cannot elect to work for God without Him calling you to this work!* Do you remember Ahab and Queen Jezebel, who was killing the ministers of Jeremiah? God punished both by killing all their family whether slave or free (1 Kings 21:21, 25–29).

The Big Five misunderstand Timothy 3:1, "This is a true saying, If a man desires the office of a bishop, he desireth a good work." The bishop is one who elects, desires, and wants to be a trainer of other ministers, priests, pastors, evangelists, and Bible teachers! Therefore, if you want to be a supervisor, trainer, or instructor, should you not be all that and more of the subordinates you wish to lead unto holiness? Can you imagine an instructor for pilots for F-14 Tomcats who have never flown an F-14 Tomcat him- or herself? *No!* So what follows verse 1 of the third chapter of Timothy are the minimum requirements for the office of a bishop—if you want to train ministers and priests, you should be the epitome of them that you lead!

Likewise, the Big Five misunderstand celibacy; it is a gift and not an election, as Paul explains in 1 Corinthians 7:7, and that it would be good if every man would be as me—I do not desire a wife! This was Paul's gift from God called celibacy because every man has his own nature as a gift from God! The Catholic Church has problems with their ministers from the outset: first, many are not "called" by God; secondly, you cannot "ask, demand, and require" a naturally heterosexual man or woman to be celibate and have no desires for the opposite sex! It is against their nature and gifts from God to ask them to be the opposite of what God has made them! Lastly, because the Big Five misunderstand these two points, they absolutely flunk the test of same-sex and homosexual education! The latter embraced a nature not given by God, and this is the reason they cannot help their deviant love for the same sex and cannot avoid the judgment of Romans 1:28, "God gave them over to a reprobate mind, to do those things which are not convenient."

We could write volumes on what God was saying to Apostle Paul here, but the God I know may be testing mankind as to how we relate to the homosexual, lesbians, and transgender community! Try on this food for thought: God hates the sin and not the sinner! God told the prophet Hosea to take back his adulterous wife on every occasion (Hosea 1:3, 3:1)! (God was comparing the adulterous wife to Israel's repeated disobedience and rebelliousness.) Why? God was showing Hosea and us something—that is, if I (God) can forgive you (mankind) for your sins on a daily basis, how come you cannot forgive each other? As one disciple asked Jesus, "Well, how many times should we forgive our brother who sins against me?" Jesus replied, "Seventy times seven!" (Matthew 18:21–22) And since no form of homosexuality is an unforgivable sin, then how can you treat your brother or sister who is homosexual with such disdain and violence of thought when the sins of you heterosexual persons are forgiven by God every day! God may be testing our response and tolerance to homosexuals by challenging us to have agape love for them although their sin is an abomination to God (Leviticus 20:13).

"Not a sermon, just a thought," says Rev. Dr. Lon Solomon from the McLean Bible Church in Northern Virginia!

Man's Church versus Women Pastors, The Chief Witness— the Word of God!

Some months ago, a dear friend and "brother by another mother" asked me to write something to persuade him and his church group that women are rightfully positioned as ministers and pastors for the gospel of Jesus Christ, or they are not! His church does not accept the proposition that women can be called by God to perform the same task as men in the gospel without running afoul of God's "golden rule" that man is head of household and no woman should usurp the authority of man! Now all of this is true, but there is one entity who can usurp the authority of man, and that is God Almighty! God can rearrange, reset, and reposition the authority of man to suit His holy purpose at any time, for any reason, and at a twinkling of an eye (1 Corinthians 15:52 KJV)!

When I first received the assignment, I first thought, *Why are we going over this issue in the twenty-first century again?* The issue was pretty much thoroughly vetted some fifteen to twenty years ago when the Presbyterian Church, USA, was embroiled in the controversy over ordaining women ministers! However, the "vetting" was pretty much done by the men, and the women mostly argued their position on civil rights grounds and not the Word of God! I first thought that I would begin and end the conversation in the New Testament with the historical account of Paul observing the women running the church at Corinth. Peter asked Him, "Should we stop them?"

Paul said, "No—they do the work of the Lord!"

Secondly, I was content to argue as if in a legal brief (being a retired lawyer and trying hard to supplant my "man ways" of doing things by embracing "God ways") the letters of Paul, who dealt with the subject quite judiciously, I thought, from the book of Romans to the book of Titus. In chapter 16 of Romans, Apostle Paul heralded the authority of Phoebe, the cofounder of the Church at Ephesus with Paul, and left her solely in charge of that church as its supreme leader! As I quoted this transition to an assistant minister of my brother's church, he retorted that being a leader in God's house does not equivocate to being pastor of God's house! At that very instance, I knew that the problem of convincing men who have swallowed the Roman Catholic view of women in the world, lock, stock, and barrel, without question, is a worthy subject to revisit through the Word of God and not through the historical lens of man!

Men are quite confident in their view of history—that is, "if that is the way it has been for all these many years, then that is the way that God has ordered it!" To conclude that that is the way it has always been cannot justify its present status. I have heard this argument a thousand times from white people who opine, "If I have not heard about this view in all of my days, then it is not a valid point!" When you question a white person with a PhD in history who has not considered that all of his/her education has been from the Eurocentric view, these people often dismiss the contributions of people of color. The inhabitants of Africa, Asia, North America, Latin America, South America, and Australia were not just sitting around doing nothing, awaiting the arrival of the white man from Europe to introduce them to "culture"!

The concomitant ignorance accompanying this view makes it even harder to discuss the Word of God with these people because they presume that "if it was to be known, then I would already know it." One must argue the orientation of the entire world against a false view of creation! How can you call yourself a Christian and dismiss God's truth that the entire civilization of man started in the fertile crescent from the Euphrates, Tigris, and Mesopotamia rivers eastward through the Garden of Eden (Genesis 2:11–14) to the shores of the Nile River in Egypt or the Land of Goshen? The history of mankind did not start in *Europe*!

So when you start off with a false premise despite all of the evidence to the contrary, and then you barrel down the road of ignorance for another two thousand years following the pathology of the councils of men (Nice, Trent, etc.), that is, the view of Roman Catholicism. It is natural that you "shipwreck" all of mankind when you fail to follow the statutes and commandments of God (Nehemiah 10:29) and then reject His will for man according to God's holy plan! When you ignore the teachings of the world's greatest modern holy men and women (Apostle Paul, Phoebe, biblical historians Josephus and others, Mohammed, Martin Luther, John and Charles Wesley, Mother Teresa, Martin Luther King, the Right Reverend Billy Graham, and others), then it is self-evident that you hold these other truths in the wrong posture! Apostle Paul writes in 2 Peter 3:16 (KJV) that "as also in all [of] his [Paul's] epistles, speaking in them of these things;" (v. 1–15) "in which are some things hard to be understood which they that are unlearned and unstable wrest, as they do also the other scriptures, unto their own destruction."

As Jesus put it to the Sadducees and Pharisees, "Why do you wash your hands before you eat bread and then you transgress against the commandments by your traditions?" (Matthew 15:1–3). Jesus was making the point that if you transgress one of the Mosaic laws, then you transgress all of them, and it is hypocrisy to not try to keep all of the laws! Men do the same with God's Word—they make it a smorgasbord where they pick and choose what they want to eat when the entire table is there for their nourishment, well-being, and enjoyment (2 Timothy 3:16). So the men that cling to this one misunderstood scripture—"suffer not a woman to teach and to usurp authority over the man, but to be in silence" (2 Timothy 2:12)—fall short of full understanding! By "leaning unto thy own understanding" (Proverbs 3:4, 5), they dismiss all of God's other evidence that

He has much more work for women to do in the ministry of the gospel of Jesus Christ! Secondly, by which they divorce themselves from God's holy plan by their own ignorance, selfishness, and blind allegiance to the "rule of men!"

God is not pleased when He sends a gift to man for his own betterment and that gift is rejected! What do you think God would have done to Adam if he had rejected Eve as his mate? Likewise, foolish men who refuse to accept the basic premise of Martin Luther (a Catholic priest and lawyer) who concluded that the "affairs of men (and women) are to be governed by the Word of God and not by the councils of men [Nice, Trent, etc.]" do hereby commit error! See 2 Peter 3:16, where it is written that men who are "unlearned and unstable" do wrest (interpret) to their own damnation not only the epistles of Peter, but as they do all Scripture! Let us put man's interpretation to test with the Word of God and His examples.

1.   *Deborah, a prophetess (Judges 4:4)*

In the fourth chapter, fourth verse, of Judges, we are introduced to Deborah, the prophetess and the wife of Lapidoth. If she is a wife, then we know that she was married to one man and pledged her love and allegiance to this man. But Deborah was also a judge as the "children of Israel came up to her for judgment" (v. 5)! God blessed Deborah with wisdom and knowledge so that she could decide disputes among her people. As in all things that God does, if it is His will for you to do something for Him, He will also give you the source, that is, the means, the tools, and the wherewithal to accomplish the task! Secondly, if Deborah is clothed with the title, she also has the authority from God and the tools whereby to do the job! Likewise, in all of the battles the children of Israel were told to wage for God, He equipped them with the necessary faith, trust, and staying power to finish off the enemy in the fashion intended!

Let us pause right here and discern God's plan to date! Deborah is a prophet just like Moses, Abraham, Joshua, Isaiah, Ezekiel, Elijah, and the like. God talked to most of His prophets face-to-face, did He not? Although the text does not recite whether He talked with

Deborah, but surely she heard from Him in her visions and dreams! Nonetheless, Deborah was a judge, a prophet, and the wife of Lapidoth. There is no mentioning here that her husband had a problem with his wife being a servant of God! Let me make this analogy: if the husband is a godly Christian man, and both he and his wife are in Christ, and the wife is the pastor of the church, and her husband is chairman of the deacon board, where is the conflict? Where is the usurpation of authority if the husband is head of the household and the wife is the pastor of his church? As long as they are living in one accord, respect each other's authority from God through the blood of Jesus Christ, and are both "willing and obedient" (Isaiah 2:19), where forth is there a problem? If the wife submits to the husband in the affairs of the home and the husband submits to his godly wife in the affairs of the church and abides by the power God has invested in his wife, where is the usurpation?

The men who have a problem with a woman as head of the church or pastor probably have some undisclosed problem with women being the boss of anything else in their life—in the family, in the community, in the area, in the nation, etc. Most men do not want to work under a female supervisor or manager or district manager or regional manager and have problems typically with a person of color having that type of authority over them, period! When Hilary Clinton threatened the presidency of the United States (POTUS) in the 2016 presidential election, a lot of men and some women objected basically to her possible ascension to that office because of her sex! The vehement objections to her policies and her handling of the Benghazi tragedy under her tutelage as Secretary of State was nothing more than a pretense.

Similarly, former president Jimmy Carter opined that following Barack Hussein Obama's nomination to POTUS 2008, most of the objections to his viewpoints and policies were based in a racial stereotype and nothing more! America was not ready to have a black man as commander in chief, and most men and a great deal of women reject a woman as pastor! According to a survey by the Pew Charitable Trust in 1997, 74 percent of the women responding to the poll still believed that a "woman's place is in the home" and, thereby, she had no business running anything except a household!

God, in His infinite wisdom, since He is all-knowing, all-seeing, and all-powerful, knew that in Christian churches one day women would attend religious services at higher rates than men (Pew Research Center 2014 U.S. Religious Landscape Study) because it is the men who have largely rebelled against God throughout the ages. Naming the women who have disobeyed God are the following: (1) Eve in the garden; (2) Miriam, the sister of Moses; (3) Queen Vashti, who tried to circumvent the power of her king Ahasuerus and refused his command to attend a party in his honor, and she was replaced as queen by Esther (Esther 1:12–15, 2:17); and (4) Queen Athaliah, who tried to kill all of the heirs to the throne before she was slain herself by order of the new king Jehoida (2 Chronicles 22:10–13, 23:14). So there are a few examples of women who defied God!

But overwhelmingly, the women who aided God's servants are numerous: (1) Rahab, the harlot who saved the lives of Joshua and Jacob and who was offered salvation with the children of Israel (Joshua 6:17); (2) Jael, Heber's wife, slew the enemy named Sisera, which sealed the victory of Deborah and Barak (Judges 4:21); (3) the two Marys—Mary Magdalene, Mary (the mother of James and Joses), and the mother of Zebedee's sons (Matthew 27:56)—who followed Jesus to the tomb and made the report that "He is risen" (Matthew 28:7); (4) mother Eunice and grandmother Lois, who instructed young Timothy in the Words of God through Christ Jesus as a child (2 Timothy 1:5–6; 3:15). How did these two women, a mother and a daughter, learn the Scriptures? They had to have been taught by someone who knew it well, and that someone could have been Jesus Himself or one of His disciples or from one of the students of the disciples. It is commonly held that Simon Peter taught John Mark the gospel of Jesus (1 Peter 5:13; Acts 15:37, 38).

Jesus's disciples were not with Him at all times, which explains why the woman at the well was able to approach Him (or He approached her since she asked Him for a drinking gourd) (John 4:4–42)! And let us consider the knowledge of Eunice and Lois, which was so specific and true! Their knowledge does not appear to be the result of a few casual meetings but the attainment of a steady dose of gospel teaching! Likewise, we have recorded thirty-four scriptures that cite the crowds around Jesus on many occasions: Luke 14:25; Mark 5:24; Matthew 8, 18; Mark 10:1; Luke 5:1; Matthew 4:25. As I said earlier, while the disciples were off buying food, medicine, or delivering a message, many people would have approached Jesus with a healing issue or spiritual advice!

2. The ordination of Phoebe by Apostle Paul

The most direct evidence of God's approval of women as ministers and as pastors besides the anecdotal evidence of Paul witnessing the women running the Church at Corinth is found in the book of Romans. Paul's coronation of Phoebe in Romans 16:1–16 recites the following: "Phoebe our sister, which is a servant of the church which is at Cenchrea; That you receive her in the Lord as becometh saints, and that ye assist her in whatsoever business she hath need of you: for she has been a succourer of many and myself also."

Let us diagnose this one powerful and revealing sentence:

1. *Our sister, Phoebe is!* She is our sister in Christ, and she is also a co-laborer with Paul (they started the Church at Ephesus together).

   Paul had already written the great letter to the Gentiles in Rome. In Romans 8:14, he opined, "For as many as are led by the Spirit of God, they are the sons of God!" Why not the sons and daughters of God? This is where we draw upon first-century history: In the days of Jesus and Paul, *papyrus* (the Greek word for *paper*) was very scarce and very valuable. The days of Gutenberg printing presses would not arrive for another 1,600 years when paper technology had become mechanized and made from a solution of tree bark and/or tree parts and then dried and pressed into form! In Jesus's day, paper was carefully shaved from tree logs by a superlong razor about four to six feet in length. The process was slow and tedious! Therefore, the writers of the

Holy Scriptures in the first century AD could not afford to always write "he and she," "sons and daughters," "male and female," and "brothers and sisters"—one word had to do for a single and sometimes a dual meaning.

This is why understanding context is vital to understanding the Bible! Any student of the Bible should read the first six pages of the American Revised Standard Version of the Bible in the section named "How to Read the Bible with Understanding." In said section, there is mentioning of this shortage of paper, which prompted the writers of the Bible to truncate some of their writing to save paper and cost. This is why the "unlearned and untrained" (2 Peter 3:16) who reject direction from other learned individuals run afoul of God's basic learning principle, that is, "lean not unto thou own understanding" (Proverbs 3:5)!

This is why God already wrote that "fools despise wisdom and instruction" (Proverbs 1:5). It is so hard for not only educated people, but for the learned (those who have been entreated by their elders and have endured wisdom) to work with those who are hostile to some of the educated and learned among them! I say to people all the time, "A man, woman, boy, or girl who already falsely presume that they know that which would have been impossible for them to learn on their own can rarely be taught!" Ignorance is simply the misfortune of not having had the opportunity to be taught. There is no shame or sin in telling anyone, "I do not know!" And sometimes those seminary graduates are a stubborn lot as well. They rub laypeople with the unjust wand of the formal process of education and tell them in no uncertain terms that "I have been to the university, and I know!" Yeah, most of our elders have gone to the Jesus School of Bible Instruction and have been taught by the High Professor called Jesus, the Christ.

This is why God instituted "the plan of learning" that was used by Jesus: He sent the disciples out in twos to spread the gospel! Then Jesus trained the Twelve and sent them out! Then the Twelve trained seventy more, and they were sent out! We have reason to believe that the book of Mark was written secondhand after he was told of the Gospel of Jesus Christ by Peter (Acts 12:12, 25 and Acts 15:37).

Apostle Paul took young Timothy, who had been instructed in the knowledge of Jesus by his mother and grandmother as a child! Paul recognized a whole lot of him in young Timothy as young Paul had been a temple worker at the Sanhedrin beginning at age eight, so he knew the customs of the Pharisees, Sadducees, and the high priests! God intended that all ministers of Jesus learn at the knee of their elders, who were taught by someone who was taught by someone who was taught by Jesus. It was never God's intent that any of His servants attend some school run by Pharisees and Sadducees and some of His most intense enemies (the high priest and the Roman Empire)! Why would God want a non-nominated man (like Ahab) to take over His divine province, that is, to instruct His servants? Did God send any of the prophets of old to some school? Did Jesus send any of His disciples to any school?

Of course, the basics of English, grammar, and math, most of us learned at a school, but I received instruction in the Bible at the knee of Rev. Phriendessa Chew (the wife of Rev. Walter Chew). She allowed me to come to her home and spend all day learning the Bible. The Catholic Church started seminaries and schools of theology, and despite their best noble intentions, their teaching method is not the procedure of God, Jesus the Christ, nor the Holy Ghost!

2. *A servant of the church!* One of the *Smith's Bible Dictionary,* aka *Dictionary of the Bible,* by Rev. F. N. Peloubet and M. A. Peloubet (rev. ed., reprint Philadelphia: John C. Winston Co., 1948), definitions of *servant* is "one who is distinguished as obedient and faithful to God or Christ" (Joshua 1:2; 2 Kings 8:19; Daniel 6:20; Colossians 4:12; 2 Timothy 2:24; Romans 16:1).

3. *Receive her in the Lord as become saints!* Paul directs all of those who are in the corporate church or the body of Christ to receive, accept, grant, and bestow favor upon Phoebe as becoming saints! Now if the great writer (commissioned by God as a chosen vessel upon me [Acts 9:15]) of the New Testament has been commanded by God to describe Phoebe as "a daughter beloved, a fellow co-laborer with me in the Gospel of Jesus Christ as become a saint," who art any man to disagree with Paul? I am astonished that any minister or pastor, typically of the male vintage who submits to the unadulterated Word of God and accepts all the rest of the Bible as true, has the unmitigated gall and temerity to reject this depiction of Phoebe as untrue or inaccurate! Who art man that you are fearful of him (Romans 9:20)? Do you recall God telling Micah to put Him on trial and bear witness against Him? And God began His cross-examination of the prophet Micah thusly: "Micah, did I need to consult you when I cast the stars and planets into the heavens? Did I need your permission to create man and woman and all things on the earth? Did I need you to approve of whom I nominate as my prophets, priests, and ministers?" *No. No. And no.* See Micah 6:3, 1–8 etc.

4. *And ye assist her in whatever business she hath need of you!* Phoebe has a pure heart and holy intentions, so much so that Apostle Paul gives her the green light that whatever she requests, demands, and asks of you, you do it! Paul grants unto Phoebe the ultimate favor through divine intervention that whatever she needs is acceptable in the sight of the Lord Jesus. How many preachers, pastors, priests, and ministers today can say that God has given them the green light? Not many because most of us do not have the holiness of Abraham, Moses, Joshua, Jacob, Job, King David, and the one Jesus extended agape love to, which was Apostle John. But Phoebe was elevated among the saints of Christ and perhaps equal to Paul.

During the Civil War, President Abraham S. Lincoln met with a group of preachers every Friday evening for dinner. One preacher prayed that God agrees with us, but President Lincoln corrected him and stated that we should pray that we agree with God! So how can we agree with God and disagree with whom God appoints as His servant? When I first met the pastor of my grandfather's (George Howard Holland) church, Evergreen Baptist in the community of Wilmington outside of the town of Palmyra, Virginia, I offered my minister's license to Pastor Justin House! Pastor House responded, "I do not need to see that—it is not my business whom God calls into His service."

It is worthy of note that none of which I observed in Romans 16 in regard to women as ministers and pastors (as leaders of the church) is relayed in any Study Bible. Phoebe is relegated to the status of deaconess, which is troubling to note, but not referred to as a minister or pastor! Paul and Phoebe were cofounders of the Church at Ephesus, and then Paul was commissioned by God to go on his first missionary journey and left Phoebe in charge. See Acts 13. If one cofounder departs and leaves another, does this not mean that the remaining cofounder is the leader of the church or is the pastor of the congregation? There is no mention in the Letter to the Romans of any deacons in the Church of Ephesus, so how could Phoebe be called a deaconess by these commentaries? (See *The Jerusalem Bible* by Alexander Jones, general editor, et al. [Garden City, New York: Doubleday & Co., Inc., 1966]; *The New Bible Commentary: Revised*, edited by D. Guthrie, J. A. Motyer, A. M. Stibbs, D. J. Wiseman [Grand Rapids, MI: Wm. B. Eerdmans Publishing Co., 1970]; *The New Testament Theology—Many Witnesses, One Gospel* by I. Howard Marshall [Downers Grove, IL: Inter Varsity Press Academic, 2004].)

Marshall sought to avoid any discussion of Phoebe and the husband-and-wife ministerial teams of chapter 16 by omitting any comment on the entire chapter! The Revised Standard Version (RSV) translates the King James Version (KJV) of the phrase "servant of the church" as "deaconess." Sadly, as much as I praise the RSV for their scrupulous attention to not translating anything out of context from the Latin Vulgate Bible to the Greek Scriptures (New Testament),

I submit that they are wrong for interpreting *servant of the church* as *deaconess*! Jesus came as servant to the people of Israel and to the Gentiles! Paul called himself a servant to the Gospel of Jesus Christ and to the Jews and the Gentiles. I do not think that Paul equated Phoebe as below him in the ministry. I submit that Paul's praise of Phoebe and others who "laid down their own necks" (Romans 16:4 et seq.) for him as equals and co-labors of the Gospel of Jesus Christ! There is no other way to receive the adulation and adoration heaped upon Phoebe, Priscilla, Aquila, Epaenetus, Mary, Andronicus and Junia, Amplias, Urbane, Appelles, and the others recited thereafter as anything else but as praise of equals—many of whom predated Paul in the Gospel of Jesus! (See verse 7, "who also were in Christ before me.")

Even the *Women's Bible Commentary* by Carol A. Newsom and Sharon H. Ringe (editors) (London: SPCK; Louisville, KY: Westminster John Knox Press, 1992) got it right, I submit! They interpret correctly the following:

> Among the persons Paul greets in Rome, nine women appear (plus Paul's mother, make ten): Prisca, Mary, Junia, Tryphaena, Tryphosa, Persis, the mother of Rufus, Paul's mother, Julia, and the sister of Nereus. Paul singles out several of them for comments: Prisca (and Aquila) for her work with Paul and for risking her life; Mary for her hard work; Junia as an apostle; Tryphaena, Tryphosa, and Persis for their labor. Nothing in Paul's comments justifies the conclusion that these women worked in ways that differed either in kind or in quantity from the ways in which men worked. Indeed, all of the individuals listed appear in tasks of ministry, a fact that needs to be taken into account in any assessment of the roles of women in early Christianity." Ibid, at page 320.

The editors of this text also agree that it was an error for the RSV to translate the KJV language *servant of the church* to *deaconess* as they misconstrued Paul's intent and the very spirit of his praise of the other co-labors of the Gospel! Unfortunately, even the commentaries that acknowledge the importance of women in the early ministry of Christianity still fall short of Paul's full import of chapter 16 of the book of Romans. (See *New Bible Commentary*, edited by G. J. Wenham, J. A. Motyer, D. A. Carson, R. T., France—21st Century Edition [Leicester, England: Inter Varsity Press; Downers Grove, IL: Inter Varsity Press, 1994], at pages 1158–1160). Paul gave the Letter to the Romans to Phoebe not only because she happened to be traveling that way, but more importantly because she was a woman whom the Roman Empire completely dismissed as a cogent being. Thereby, it was relatively safe for her to carry this most important document to the believers in Rome. Paul understood this weakness of the Roman Empire and, thereby, he utilized the covert potential of women to carry, spread, and preserve the Gospel of Jesus!

Paul's wisdom was amplified by the unction of the Holy Ghost to employ all of these women in very strategic places and times in furtherance of the plan of God to not allow man to subvert, usurp, or divert the Gospel of Jesus Christ! God, Jesus, and the Holy Ghost knew that centuries later that the Word of God would be held by unrighteous men and women. These misguided and selfish miscreants would incur the wrath of God (Romans 1:18), and they would be treacherous to the letter, the spirit, and the bearer of the Word. No rational male minister can deny that God has called women to the ministry of Jesus Christ! And this calling was not by default as Peter was supposed to have forsaken the Jews and extended the spirit of fellowship to the Gentiles (Acts 15:7). The inclusion of women as bearers of the Word of God began eons ago, and it is rooted in God's master plan!

3.   *The husband-and-wife ministerial team division (Romans 16:3–27)*

Apostle Paul's tribute to these husband-and-wife ministerial teams begins with his salute of Priscilla and Aquila (v. 3). It is also a clear indication of the risk of death that these people suffered for their work for the Gospel of Jesus Christ! Paul was a hunted man, and anyone who assisted him was risking arrest, torture, and death! The reference to Phoebe being a succorer was not only of the church (the gospel of Jesus Christ), but of Paul as well. The risk is twofold: (1) to work in the ministry of Jesus by oneself (2) and then to assist anyone else who is being hunted by the high priests (the Sanhedrin) and the Roman soldiers. Our first introduction to Aquila and Priscilla is in Acts, the eighteenth chapter. Paul first met them on his way from Athens (in Greece) to Corinth (v. 1), and we know that Corinth had a congregation that was being run by women. So it was not "unusual" for a woman to be prominent in the Church at Corinth. We learn that the husband, Aquila, is a Jew from Pontus, and he and his wife (Priscilla) have recently traveled from Italy. Emperor Claudius had recently expelled all of the troublesome Jews from Rome and the Roman Empire (v. 2).

And verse 3 is very much overlooked and underappreciated by Christians today: "And because he [Aquila] was of the same craft, he [Paul] abode with them, and wrought: for by their occupation they were tentmakers."

Netmakers are very much necessary to the fishing industry as the commercial fishermen were not line-and-pole fishermen. They were net fishermen who would pitch their tents anywhere along the shore where the fish are taken to quickly process and ship fresh fish to the market and to their customers. And tentmakers and netmakers tended to "run together" as their trades complemented each other. Both trades were necessary to complement the net fisherman who needed shade (a tent) and people to mend their nets.

Now, some of Jesus's disciples were net menders (Mark 1:19) and tentmakers, so it would not arise any suspicion that this group of men was found together at many times during the day and the night. This cover or the ruse of being fishers of men (Mark 4:19) belied their dual occupation as tentmakers. That they were first purveyors of the Gospel of Jesus of Christ was an ingenious device by God! He planted Jesus among a group of men who were always moving around bodies of water (Sea of Galilea, the Jordan River, the Aegean

Sea, the Red Sea, etc.) and frequenting port cities. These men lived and traveled about under the radar of Roman soldiers—they were ordinary or "dry long so" or "hath no form nor comeliness" (Isaiah 53:2), just as Jesus was described by the prophet Isaiah.

They were not the only group of people that did not raise any suspicion from the Pharisees, the Sadducees, and Roman soldiers. The women were equally devalued by the Romans and the high priests. The Roman Empire was very much misogynistic in nature. They lauded women with praise for their beauty and booty (in a sexist physical sense), but not for their brains and spiritual heart. They completely dismissed the craftiness of women to manipulate men who underestimated their powers of persuasion! Throughout the Old Testament, it was the women who schmoozed, tricked, and manipulated men into doing or suggesting stupid stuff, such as Eve, Job's wife, and Joseph's wife, to name a few.

It did not stop when the Romans came to Jerusalem in the New Testament. The following are good examples of women exhibiting great influence over men: Herod's daughter tricked her father into delivering the head of John the Baptist to her (Matthew 14:6–11); Pontius's wife warned her husband to reject the business of crucifying a righteous man (Jesus) to pacify the high priest (Matthew 27:19) (he could have spared Jesus's life and settled the entire matter quickly); the little girl that unmasked Peter as a confidant of Jesus; etc. (Matthew 26:69–70).

Now, back to Aquila and Priscilla (Acts 18). There is no recorded episode where Paul opposed the theology of this husband-and-wife ministerial team, but when Silas and Timotheus came from Macedonia (v. 5), the arguing started (Paul was preaching to the Jews that Christ was Jesus and circumcision was no longer necessary)! Paul became so pressed in the spirit (v. 5) that he abandoned the gospel to the Jews and Greeks (v. 4) and declared that "henceforth I will go unto the Gentiles" (v. 6)! It is pretty much accepted that Aquila and Priscilla were into the Jesus movement long before Paul!

The timeline agrees with this assessment: Jesus began His earthly ministry around AD 32 to 34 and was spreading His teaching long before Saul (Paul) was blinded by this intense light along the road to Damascus around AD 48 to 51 or so! So while Paul was still persecuting the Jews, Eunice and Lois, Priscilla and Aquila, and others were in Christ before Paul (Romans 16:7)! They had learned the Gospel of Jesus Christ, and they were spreading it in their travels. From this passage in Acts 18, we can see that the Gospel of Jesus Christ had spread to Rome long before Paul's first defense of the Gospel in Italy by letter! By the time Paul arrived, the situation in Rome was near the boiling point, and Emperor Claudius had had enough of these Jews. Not long thereafter, Paul was freed from his prison cell by divine intervention (Acts 16:25, 26)!

4. *The husband-and-wife ministerial teams of Romans 16:1 et seq.*

Paul took the time to name these husband-and-wife ministerial teams as a tribute to Priscilla and Aquila, who embraced Paul while he was in Cenchrea as a brother beloved. Paul had a vow from God to teach the Gospel of Jesus Christ to not only to the Jews who would not listen, but to any Gentile as well (Acts 18: 18)! Paul sailed into Syria with Priscilla and Aquila, a righteous couple, as a "testament" of their importance to the missionary journey of the gospel! It is clear to me and my research that Paul was making a statement that would endure for the ages: God has great need for these righteous couples, and they will do great work for the kingdom of Jesus Christ.

a. In verse 4, Paul recites the importance of Priscilla and Aquila that they laid down their necks for his life, for which he gives thanks. They also saved the gospel from perishing if there was an untimely death of Paul. The churches of the Gentiles owe their survival to them who were in Christ before him. Without Priscilla and Aquila saving Paul from certain death, the gospel to the Gentiles would have not happened as fully as it did! In verse 5, Paul continues, "Likewise greet the church that is in their house." Paul did not say greet the church in their house with Aquila as the pastor and his wife, Priscilla, as his helpmate or assistant pastor or deaconess! Paul meant the church that they ran together!

b.   In verse 7, Paul "salute(s) Andronicus and Junta, my kinsmen and my fellow prisoners; they are men of note among the apostles and they were in Christ before me." This husband-and-wife team learned Christ from the apostles of Jesus or from Jesus Himself (the text does not specify). If Christ had a precise instruction not to inform women of this faith, then the apostles did not do a good job of keeping this Jesus movement away from them! It is the women who were instrumental to spreading the gospel because the Pharisees, the high priest of the Sanhedrin, and the Roman soldiers did not suspect the women were informing the public of Jesus! They were the least equipped, the most ignored, and the most unsuspecting of Jesus's teachers as they were not men! (In verses 5, 6, 8–11, Paul lists some single people who have done great work for the Lord.)

c.   In verse 12, Paul salutes Tryphena and Tryphosa, who labor in the Lord.

d.   In verse 13, Paul calls our attention to "Rufus chosen in the Lord, his mother and mine." These are three people whom Paul says were chosen in the Lord—that is, these people have been chosen by Christ to spread the gospel as Apostle Paul was chosen by Jesus as "a vessel unto the Lord" (Acts 9:15). A lot of church organizations do not subscribe to the calling principle of the Bible—that is, God will call any persons into His service at any age and at any time. We have proof here that He has called these three people.

In the book of Romans, Paul recites in chapter 8, verses 28–30 that "God calls those according to His purpose…for whom he did foreknow, he also did predestinate to be conformed to be the image of his Son, that he might be the firstborn among many brethren. Moreover, whom he did predestinate, them he also called; and whom he called, them he also justified; and whom he justified, them he also glorified." Is there any doubt that God called the "apostles, prophets, evangelists, pastors, and teachers" (Ephesians 4:11) and He sends them to wherever He needs them?

Lastly, in verse 13, there is a huge clue as to God's and Paul's methodology: God called Rufus's mother and Paul's mother, who are not named! Neither one of these women are named because of security reasons. If their names were to be found in print, the Romans would find them and torture them to reveal Paul's whereabouts! The Roman soldiers (nor the Roman Empire) nor the high priests paid any attention to women moving about, doing their mundane chores of laundering, going to the market, accompanying their husbands to one place or another, or even visiting the temple at Jerusalem, where the women were not allowed to mix in with the men.

Therefore, the women were perfect vessels to spread the gospel of Jesus; they were not under suspicion, they blended into the landscape, and they had no formal power in the Roman Empire! They could not vote or participate in the Roman government or in the governance of the Sanhedrin or of the local province. So it was a natural cover for Paul's mother and Rufus's mother to be in Christ even before Paul—the foundation of the gospel had already been laid. So while Paul was at the Sanhedrin since he was eight years old, his mother came into contact with someone spreading the gospel of Jesus Christ! This foundation laid the protection network for Paul's future ministry as there was help all along his journeys from the most insignificant people in the land besides the poor people of the hinterlands, that is, the women!

My last observation: how did all of these women (Eunice and Lois, Phoebe, Aquila, Typhena, Tryphosa, Paul's mother, Rufus's mother, etc.) come in contact with the gospel of Jesus Christ and then get intense training in this new religious experience? Surely, one cannot conclude that all of this was by accident!

Now Jesus had already established that if you possess the gospel, you are duty bound to spread it (Matthew 28:19)! In Matthew 5, verses 13 through 16, our Lord and Savior expresses His desire, hope, and command that we believers are the salt of the earth. Salt is used to preserve things or less it has no other purpose (v. 13)! Jesus commanded His followers to evangelize the entire earth with

His gospel. And, the best way to do this was to spread His message among as many ethnic groups, cultures and languages as possible by knowledgeable men and women.

Likewise, since all these women had the Gospel, Jesus, their boss, wanted them to distribute it among the people: "Ye are the light of the world. A city that is set on a hill cannot be hid" (v. 14). "Neither do men light a candle, and put it under a bushel [basket], but on a candlestick; and it giveth light unto all that are in the house" (v. 15). This clear mandate of the gospel is still very hard to teach in today's climate—too many believers of the twenty-first century take this lightly (the Word of God) and become arrogant, possessive, and stingy with it. So much so to the point that many do not wish to share it with others, as Jesus commands us in Matthew 28:19, 20. He said, "Go ye therefore, and teach all nations, baptizing them in the name of the Father, and of the Son, and of the Holy Ghost: Teaching them to observe all things whatsoever I have commanded you: and, lo, I am with you always, even unto the end of the world" (v. 20).

This is one reason that the Word of God is suffering setbacks (or slow advancement) around the globe! Too many of the men and women God has entrusted (Matthew 7:6) with the Word have become bigheaded, haughty, and vain-seeking, seeking only to fill their bellies and greed. They have used the Word of God for ungodly purposes, such as the Pharisees and Sadducees did by making the people slaves unto them and other men and not of God!

If you do not spread the gospel with your faith, loving-kindness (Galatians 5:22 et seq.), generosity, good works, spiritual advice (2 Timothy 3:16), and so forth, you have done a disservice to the Word of God! If you keep it within thyself for selfish reasons, you are not a light unto men! A few churches teach that we are all ministers of the gospel, and that is true to the extent that we are all called to spread the Word of God, but all that spread the Word have not been called to preach the Word of God in the sense of Romans 10:14 (c), "And how shall they hear without a preacher?"

I submit that if God and/or His apostles, prophets, evangelists, pastors, and teachers (Ephesians 4:11) allowed women to hear the Gospel of Jesus Christ, then God ordained it so, and God wishes women to preach the Gospel as well! It is as clear as night and day that God wanted this to happen, that God allowed this to happen, and that God has purposed this to happen to preserve the Gospel of Jesus for mankind for all future generations! God does not make any mistakes, and He can use all things for His good and perfect will (Romans 12:2)!

Likewise, Jesus asks the question in Luke 6:46, "Why call ye me Lord, and do not the things which I say?" All of the sin, corruption, mayhem, violence, and unrighteousness that is in the world is due to our collective disobedience (Romans 1:23–32, 28). Just imagine how God feels about one servant rejecting another servant. Suppose Moses had rebuked Joshua as God's appointed successor to the former. Suppose the people had rejected Deborah as Israel's prophet, king, and military leader. Suppose Paul had not used the women to conceal, preserve, and deliver the gospel to the Gentiles by transporting it to Rome. In just about every aspect of God's plan, mankind has frustrated His holy purpose!

Could the rejection of women as purveyors of the gospel be another major disobedience to God's plan? How come some men are so hell-bent to defy God? How come men today will not submit to the wisdom of "Gamaliel, a doctor of the law (who) had in reputation among all the people" (Romans 5:34, 35–39)? Gamaliel reasoned that if these men who bear the gospel of Jesus are not sent by God, then "this counsel or this work be of men, it will come to nought" (v. 38). "But if it be of God, ye cannot overthrow it; lest haply ye be found even to fight against God" (v. 39). The same analogy could apply to women—if men kick against the gospel of Jesus Christ being preached by women, could they be unknowingly fighting against God?

On the day of Pentecost, where the obscure Jesus movement was first launched as a world ministry (Acts 1:13), Peter recorded that when they were coming in, they went to an upper room, where the followers of Jesus abode. Verse 14 is a key ingredient that "these all continued with one accord in prayer and supplication, with the women and Mary, the mother of Jesus and with his brethren." These men and women who were the foundation of the Jesus movement began their worldwide ministry together on the day of Pentecost!

Who am I to tell God whom to call, whom to assemble, and whom to send? He has already spoken!

Marriage Vows Revisited

The Holy Ghost prodded me to relook at the marriage vows for another nugget of understanding! Earlier in this treatise, I looked at some husband-wife teams where both were ministers (Aquila and Priscilla); and in the Old Testament, we found the wife was the prophetess/minister (Deborah) and her husband, Lapidoth, was a non-minister! Then we dealt considerably with the husband-wife ministerial teams that Paul proffers to us in chapter 16 of Romans! But let us look at the vows that God prescribed that man has incorporated into a set of marriage vows:

1. Genesis 2:24: "Therefore shall a man leave his father and his mother, and shall cleave unto his wife: and they shall be one flesh."
2. Ephesians 5:31: "For this cause shall a man leave his father and mother, and shall be joined unto his wife, and they two shall be one flesh."
3. Ephesians 5:33: "Nevertheless let every one of you in particular so love his wife even as himself; and the wife [see] that she reverence [her] husband."
4. 1 Peter 3:7: "Likewise, ye husbands, dwell with [them] according to knowledge, giving honour unto the wife, as unto the weaker vessel, and as being heirs together of the grace of life; that your prayers be not hindered."

5. 1 Corinthians 7:3–11: "Let the husband render unto the wife due benevolence: and likewise also the wife unto the husband."

Now if you consider all these scriptures together, it is clear that God is really talking about husband and wife as being one spiritual entity or body! And being such coheirs to the kingdom (1 Peter 3:7 [b]), then where is the problem if the wife is the pastor and the husband is the chair of the deacon or trustee board? They are spiritually one. Or even reverse that—if the husband is the pastor and the wife is a deaconess, they are clothed with the same spirit in both positions! Compare this analogy to the Trinity: Jesus is God in the flesh (John 14:17), or Jesus is the embodiment of God wrapped into the flesh, and it is Jesus who sent the Holy Ghost as our comforter to assist us while He is away from earth! So why is it so difficult for men to accept the notion of two physical bodies (man and woman) becoming spiritually one in Christ?

Afterword

In the Last Days

In the book of Joel, chapter 2, verses 28 and 29, the prophet wrote the following:

> And, it shall come to pass, that I will pour out my spirit upon all flesh: and your sons and daughters shall prophesy, you old men shall dream dreams, young men shall see visions: And also upon servants, and upon the handmaids in those days will I pour out my spirit.

Merriam-Webster's Dictionary defines *prophesy* as the following:

> (transitive verb) 1) to utter by or as if by divine inspiration; 2) to give instruction in religious matters: preach; 3) to make prediction

Paul recalls Joel's passage in Acts 2:17–18 with a little more urgency: "And it shall come to pass in the last days, saith God, I will pour out my Spirit upon all flesh: and your sons and daughters shall prophesy, and your young men shall see visions and your old men shall dream dreams. And on my servants and on my handmaidens I will pour out in those days of my Spirit: and they shall prophesy." It would appear that when God starts calling the daughters and the handmaidens to prophesy, to preach, and to declare His Word, time is wrapping up, and this calling is a sign that the end-times are near (2 Timothy 3:1).

Previously in this book, I have argued that God has always had a purpose, a plan, and a mission for women in the ministry of Jesus Christ. Some men of this world have been active in the campaign to prevent women from serving God righteously and, thusly, have interfered with God's plan for over two thousand years! It is clear from Joel to Acts that when God starts calling all His children to prophesy, time is wrapping up and the last days are near unto hand! (Even if that time is hundreds of years in the future, it is much closer now than at the beginning of Jesus's ministry [AD 32 to 35].) God has told us to look for these signs that reveal His plans to us and give us keys to His revelations. You cannot discover these signs unless you are a serious believer and a diligent searcher of God's Word! Remember the question Jesus asked the Pharisees, "Have you searched the Scriptures like the Bereans?" (Acts 17:10, 11). Searching the Scriptures like the Bereans is a little beyond "studying to show thyself approved" (2 Timothy 3:16), which gets you a passing grade from God! But doing a diligent search of the Scriptures is the nature of a seasoned veteran for Christ. As Paul describes in Hebrews 5: 10–14, the high priest called of God after the Order of Melchizedek (v. 10) had many things to say, some hard to be uttered to the dull of hearing.

The hard things are difficult for the near-the-well minister to say, let alone teach! If the pastor has not taught his flock the hard things steadily and incrementally, then it would be more difficult to discern these hard things. Paul refers to these things as strong meat in Hebrews 5, and the seasoned Christians ought to be on strong meat (the most searing wisdom of Scripture) after a term of years! If you have been dutifully attending Sunday school and Bible study and studying diligently on your own, you should have been weaned off of milk and receiving the sincere meat of the Word! After ten to twenty years of this regimen, you should be ready for strong meat.

The degree of difficulty of your development from churchgoer to Hebrews 5:12 is the following: (a) Jesus says to His disciples in 2 Peter 2:12, "As newborn babies desire the sincere milk of the word, this is how I will feed you that 'ye may grow thereby'"; (b) you must "study to show thyself approved" (2 Timothy 2:16), not just reading it to satisfy a lesson plan; (c) you must "continue thou the things which thou hast learned which are able to make thee wise unto salvation through faith which is in Christ Jesus" (2 Timothy 3:14, 15). Thereby, realizing that "all Scripture is given by inspiration of God, and is profitable for doctrine, for reproof, for correction, for instruction in righteousness" by applying the Word of God in your daily living! I call part c the great struggle in all of our lives, even in mine as well.

I cannot predict how this book will impact male and female preachers. The truth is often elusive in today's environment of super-fast search engines and technological advances. Who or what do you believe or trust? I pray that the reader, if originally skeptical of my theology, allows it some time and space to grow in your mind and heart! If this theology is true, then it comes from the Word of God! All I did was stumble upon it among God's many wonders and truisms!

About the Author

The author grew up in a small rural village called Cismont, Virginia, near the City of Charlottesville. He was active in several sports in high school and continued in track and field in college at Princeton University (1972–1976). He joined his local church at the age of twelve. After graduating from law school at the University of Virginia (1980), he joined his first Bible study as an adult. He had quite a few women as his teachers in Bible study and Sunday school in the last forty years. Subsequently, in 1992, he was licensed as a Baptist preacher at his home church of Zion Hill Baptist. His training as a minister was greatly augmented by several women pastors and teachers who took the time and agape love to instruct him properly. To be sure, he has made his share of mistakes and sins in his adult life, for which he begs forgiveness from God, Jesus, and the Holy Spirit. He transitioned from the active practice of law in 1996 to consulting and legal drafting to allow more time for his ministry and writing. He has to his credit many articles and stories in several newspapers and magazines, but he has written more than a few editorials for the *Vinegar Hill Magazine* in Charlottesville, Virginia, in the last eight years where he now resides. The Rev. Dr. Bates is a divorcee and is a step-grandfather to more than six children who call him *Papa*.